dalus Press

editor John F Deane

THE MYTH OF THE SOUTH

by

CIARAN O'DRISCOLL

The Dedalus Press
24 The Heath
Cypress Downs
Dublin 6W
Ireland

ISBN 1 873790 09 0

This is number *76* of an edition of 300 copies

Typesetting: Peanntrónaic Teo.
BÁC 14. 01-904265
Printed in Ireland by Colour Books Ltd.

Cover design by Niamh Foran

The Dedalus Press receives financial assistance from
An Chomhairle Ealaíon, The Arts Council, Ireland

THE MYTH OF THE SOUTH

1. The Myth of the South

It is true that in the South there is, in general,
an absence of agency – I mean of the efficient sort.
Things somehow *get* done, if you know what I mean.
But things could just as easily *not* get done.
Things *happen* according to the seasons,
and even then they depend on mood, which depends
in turn on the weather. The people of the South –
even in bigger towns, such as Li-Chung and Li-Cho –
lack any sense of urgency, they haven't yet
pulled themselves out of the benignly lazy state
that natural cycles warrant in a generous climate.
(Apples taste sweeter in the orchards round Li-Cho
than anywhere on earth. The children's cheeks
are as rosy as the cheeks of the apples.)
When the Emperor comes on his five-yearly visit
there's something of a flurry, but it would look
to Northerners like a Day of Rest: people can be seen
out painting their houses or fixing wagon wheels;
again, of course, depending on the weather.
The women are more beautiful in the South;
sensuous, fun-loving, they make bad secretaries;
not that there's much need of secretaries
in Li-Chung or Li-Cho. It's said the healthy lustre

of Southern people's skin comes from bathing under
the many waterfalls, which they do all day in good
    weather.
Very few people here except state functionaries –
usually recruited from the North – are able to write:
poetry is indistinguishable from song, although
the songs have the epic quality of being endless,
which suits the temperament and is indifferent
to the weather: when they can't sing out of doors,
in their traditional wine-gardens, they sing indoors,
in their traditional wine-taverns. The one thing
they do with great gusto is to sing.
Singing has no social function of the kind
the Emperor's anthropologists seem to think
must be latent under any manifest activity;
there's no *hiatus* between life and singing,
but that is not to say, as might be said
by one of our pretentious litterateurs,
hell-bent on poetry as celebration,
that singing is life for them, as life is singing.
Between songs, there's always a period
for conversation, or in the case of wakes,
for silence. New songs are composed
almost every day, and either enter the repertoire
or don't: the only critics are the singers,
which means the people, whose final verdict
is to sing or not to sing. This may all strike you
as being egregiously *mindless,* as it did me at first,
but I found out that they discuss their songs
with one another in the throes of composition
rather than *post factum,* and they say,
Better to make sure the wine is good
than to drink it and make a bitter face.
In this way, they ensure that very few
of the songs composed are dropped as unsingable,

and it means that their repertoire is infinite
and that everything that happens is sung about,
as well as the possible and the fantastic;
their political debates, even, occur
as an exchange of songs. Apart from that,
and the apples, the naked bodies under waterfalls,
the apple-cheeked children, the births, the funerals,
the slow creaking of cartwheels towards the huge
granaries of Li-Chung and Li-Cho; as I said,
apart from beauty and ease, love, death, and apple-wine,
nobody *does* anything here in the South;
things somehow *get* done, if you know what I mean.

2. The Myth of the Capital

At this stage, as we take the air nightly
along the battlements of the Plague Wall, we hear
persistent rumours that the country is well again;
or at least its greater part; these rumours come
from the alcoholic wretches who are denied entry,
shouting from the bottom of the granite face
out of the rags and tatters of hearsay,
speaking of the second city and even the third,
where they say builders are busy and trade and
        commerce
thriving: they have heard new songs, they say,
and their feeble renditions float up to us
full of *hopes* and *loves* and *prides;* many of them
appear to be songs of building, and sound almost –
well – accomplished; a source of much amusement
as we take the air on the ramparts of the Plague
after dinner, before theatre or recital.
There is *so much* happening in the capital
these days, especially with the strolling players
and troubadours confined within the walls,
it is scarcely possible to chronicle all
that happens in one night, let alone a year.
With each new songster on the street, each new jester

or troup of wits appearing in the halls,
the importance of living in this place and time
becomes more evident. Surrounded by such ramparts,
the capital has defined itself against the country
which, ravaged by plague, may send its deceitful
emissaries no further than the butt
of this granite face on whose flat forehead we walk,
the post-prandial arbiters of taste, with our high task
of myth-making and exclusion, discrimination.
Rumours persist, as rumours will, of well-being
no further from us than a bumsore day's journey,
but by remaining wisely within these walls,
we not only protect outselves from contamination –
which were surely a selfish thing, could it be shown
with any certainty that these fables,
coming from desperate adventurers, had some substance –
but rather we protect our high office, which is,
as I said, taste and discrimination,
and the embattled ascendancy of the capital.

3. *Fragment of an Account of the North*

    ... a brief blaze of corn
in the middle of the year, like nothing else.
A sudden busyness of people harvesting,
when all the feuding is forgotten
under the Sign of the Melting Glacier. In spring
the lost possessions tumble out of melting ice;
inventories are made at that time of the year;
the next of kin of swallowed, regurgitated houses
are informed and travel through sudden valleys
to claim their own: the neatly-tagged, preserved bodies
are quickly buried, and the mourners make the Sign
of the Melting Glacier on their foreheads, and then
get down to the serious business of haggling
about who owns what; but in that brief good season
under the Sign of the Sun, the distribution
is resolved with good humour and great precision;
as if, indeed, the sight of water filling the hollows
tempered their spirits to gentleness, as if the hard
core and rumble and lack of giving way, the issue
resolved only by groan and crack and fissure,
were a thing of the long dead.
Whence, in every Northern head,
a dream of the short season of impartial weights

and measures, of the time when plenty warrants
justice and generosity; their passion
for administration and their objective eye
being no more than a dream of the sun,
which they carry with them wherever they go.
As for those who stay at home, they speak hard words
the rest of the year, and reconstitute themselves
into the ancient battle lines of ice and land.
And their poetry, written under the threat
of the Glacier, is solid and hard and pitiless
as blue ice, sharp as icicles; sometimes it has
a kind of mad humour aimed at nothing,
like a man laughing to himself in his shack
in the heart of winter, under the influence
of an immature distillation of barley ...

4. News from the Capital

What kinds of feelings are left smouldering now
in the hearths of the hearts of the population
of the Capital?
The great questions have been
exhausted by thunderous answers,
and being for the thousandth time
reasserts itself as a dull pain.
There's nothing new,
no new exciting rhythm to infer
from the many scrolls or broadsheets
they're bringing out each day under the wall
where the market gathers now –
under the Wall of Scrolls
as it's come to be called,
each parchment dense in a double sense
of crammed with hieroglyphs and packed
with profundities – under the Wall
where apples from the South and all
the suspect gew-gaws of the North are sold;
from these places where a plague
is said to rage come scant
luxuries of merchants
to whom gatekeepers turn,

with connivance of the authorities,
the blindest of blind eyes.
And children play ball against the Wall
beside the Old Cathedral of Sighs,
chased by demented deacons of sorrow,
under the Wall where the Hall
of Faiths has opened a restaurant
serving a tea imported from
the dominant creed's motherland;
the sweetest tea by acclamation
of the scriveners' feet, and not a seat
for such unlikely hacks as me
who believe in telling the truth
once in a while, when the fit
is on them, knowing the city has gone to seed
from the absence of good commerce with
the country, and a few mandarins
are sustaining this predicament
for fear of surrendering their status,
which is founded on a fiction of disease:
call it the Fall, as they do in the Hall,
or the Plague, as they do in the Chambers,
or, as the scriveners do, the Nameless Affliction,
since it rhymes with their fey sense of dereliction
or their general lack of conviction.
Children play ball against the Wall
with the same indefatigability
as scriveners scrawl out their scrolls
under the Wall, as edicts to circumvent
the infiltration of the Plague
are passed in the Chambers of the embers
of good government, as tea in endless gallons drips
from the blocked spouts of teapots into the cups
of the wraiths in the Hall of Faiths,
and there's prayer for deliverance in the air

around the Old Cathedral of Sighs,
and no one really lives, though no one dies.

5. The Myth of the North

This Northern thing goes back a long time,
necessity was the mother of our invention.
The scrawny fruit-begrudging trees, the soil
that was tundra for half the year. And so on.
(The last thing any Northerner wants to do is whine.)
We had to survive or die, and as a result,
we more than survived. We became sharper than all.
And if we possess any talent that
gives people pleasure but is of no earthly use,
such as poetry or music, we don't revel in it,
as Southerners do, for its own sake, but have the sense
to surround it with an aura of mystique,
literally to *manage* it in the only way
such ephemera can be usefully handled,
by withholding it and spreading deliberate rumours
about its excellence until someone
of great consequence, who has everything else,
has got to hear of it and thinks his life
will be dull without it. In this way our poetry
is held more in esteem than Southern singing,
which is on the lips of every Liu and Li,
though the poetry is no better than the singing.
(In fact, our best judges say privately,

and off the record, that the songs are more *inspired*.)
It is of the essence of our people
that they can convert something useless into bread;
hence the famous story of the Northerner who rented
his land for *half* the year to a Southerner.
Already, we occupy the vast majority
of positions in the administration
outside the capital. It is only a matter of time
before the scales of beleaguerment fall from the eyes
of the government and they see how much they need us.
In the end, our total control of the land
will happen by default, through our being what we are
due to our unpropitious climate, and through the fact
that fruit has always dropped into the others' mouths.

6. The Song of the Rotten Apple

Here let me sing among the cartwheels
on the side of the road to the ruined cities
where a plague of being forgotten lays
the land to waste, and a singer
no longer listened to
knows no difference between
the silence of his song
and the silence before and after.

Let me sing of this new word, *tension*,
a warp in people's shoulders;
neither to bloom nor fade
but be indeterminate, and wait
for something that never happens;
desire outrageously solidified,
a tower trying to penetrate
the empty air.

Here is a listless city that grew fat
in its own eyes, out of time.
Where the great songs were sung
to the creaking of cartwheels
and piled in the mind's granaries,

a plenty as endless
as water over waterfalls
on bright bodies.

This is not like an old song
going from quietness to quietness.
This is a song that has begun
out of the silence of the unheard
to end a shout in the night
from a warped face.
And between the silence and the shout,
a plague of events that happen by stealth.

And this is neither a song
of pillage nor of murder.
This is a song of cartwheels
that fall from carts and are not replaced,
and the slow rotting of grain
that has been gathered.
A song of the blight that infects the eye
of power: the Song of the Rotten Apple.